How to use this book

This book is divided into three parts. The cover and centre colour pages form the pirate ship. The black and white pages of figures, sea creatures and other things are for you to pull out, colour in and cut out. The other colour pages are full of history about pirates, life on a pirate ship as well as fun activities. Don't pull the colour pages out. There is a glossary on the inside back cover to help you to understand special pirate words.

Open the cover into a triangle. Fold the smaller flap over the book and push the ship tabs into the slots. Place on a flat surface.

Attach the side bits to each end of the ship.

Slot the sails and flag on top.

Colour the pictures before cutting them out.

To store, fold the side flaps inwards and close the book.

Keep all the cutouts in an envelope and tuck this into the book.

Templates

Tape a piece of tracing paper over the template or image. Trace in pencil.

Turn the tracing paper over and scribble over the lines with a pencil.

Turn over again and tape on to card or paper. Re-trace firmly over the lines. Remove tracing paper.

What are pirates?

Pirates were robbers who sailed on the sea. They attacked and stole from other ships and people along coastlines, all over the world.

Pirates used to creep up on bigger sailing ships which were heavy and slow-moving, and take them over. They called people who weren't sailors LANDLUBBERS.

A pirate would climb up into the CROW'S NEST of his ship and look through a telescope. If he saw a ship on the horizon, they would follow it. Sometimes pirates would trick ships into thinking they were harmless by flying a friendly flag (hiding the JOLLY ROGER). When it drew close, the pirates would throw a GRAPPLING IRON onto the other ship and pull it alongside so they could jump aboard.

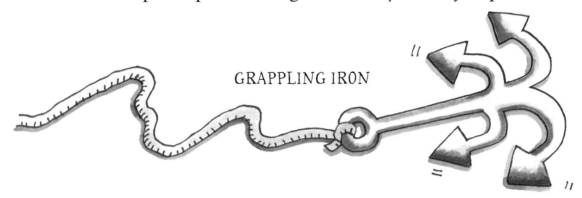

GRAPPLING IRON

Pirates were fierce and frightening – they would let out bloodcurdling cries and yells as they attacked.

Once they had captured a ship, pirates would steal everything – weapons, clothes, valuable BOOTY and the cargo the ship had been carrying, such as sugar, tobacco or cloth. All the crew would either be killed or taken prisoner. Sometimes pirates even stole the ship.

Dressed to kill

Pirates usually had only one set of clothes which they never took off. They would replace them by stealing newer ones. Most pirates didn't wear shoes.

Pirates came from countries as far apart as China, India and America and the clothes they wore depended on what the climate was like. From sweltering heat to freezing stormy seas – choose a pirate outfit from these ideas!

Make a turban and sash out of thin, colourful fabric. Wear loose pyjama trousers and a dressing gown.

Wear jewellery, waistcoats, stripey T-shirts, cut-off jeans.

Tie a scarf around your head or neck.

Find a hat with feather. Draw on a moustache.

Wear a belt over your shoulder. Draw some tattoos.

Weapons

Pirates would fire cannonballs and throw fire bombs and grenades at a trading ship until its wooden hull and canvas sails caught fire. They would also use MUSKETS to fire from a distance.

Once the pirate ship had drawn alongside, the pirates would leap on to the deck and start hand-to-hand fighting, using flint-lock pistols, CUTLASSES, swords and pikes (a type of spear).

Life on board ship

Everyone on board a pirate ship had to obey the ship's code of conduct, a set of rules designed to keep everything on board running smoothly.

In charge was the **captain**. He gave orders during battles and decided where to sail, using CHARTS.

The **quartermaster** was second in command. Only he was allowed to whip a man using a CAT O' NINE TAILS. His job was also to share out any stolen booty.

The **carpenter** was responsible for repairs to the ship and would carve a wooden leg to strap to a stump if a pirate lost a leg.

The **surgeon** sometimes had to saw off arms and legs when a man was badly injured.

The **cook** had to disguise the taste of mouldy food by using spices. They kept hens on board to provide eggs and fresh meat. They sometimes caught fish and turtles to cook.

When there was nothing else to eat, pirates ate HARD TACK (the ship's biscuits). When there was no fresh water, they drank RUM. A lot of pirates suffered from SCURVY.

The ordinary seamen shared all the jobs on board ship. The days were divided up into four-hour WATCHES when they would take turns to steer the ship and watch out for land and dangers such as rocks and other ships. When they were not working, pirates would gamble using cards or dice.

Colour the figures and other things and cut them out. You can cut close to the line if you don't want to follow it exactly. Bend the flaps back along the dotted line and stand up. If you'd like to make more, use the template instructions on the first page.

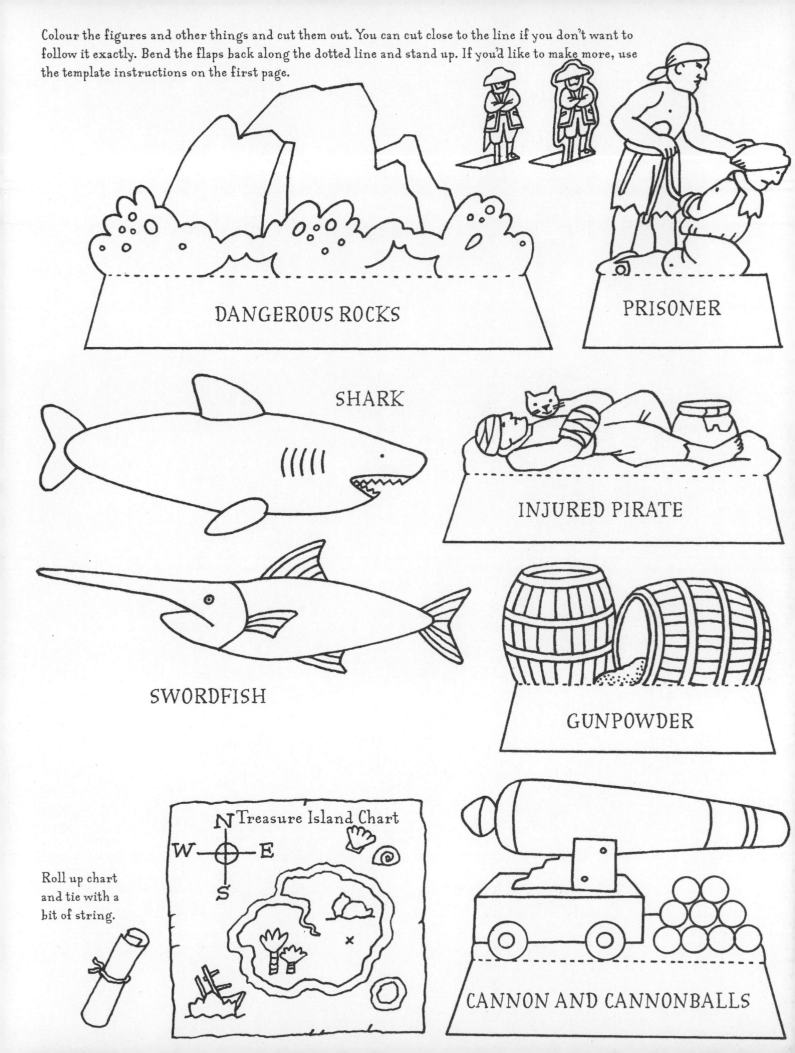

DANGEROUS ROCKS

PRISONER

SHARK

INJURED PIRATE

SWORDFISH

GUNPOWDER

Roll up chart and tie with a bit of string.

Treasure Island Chart

N
W — E
S

CANNON AND CANNONBALLS

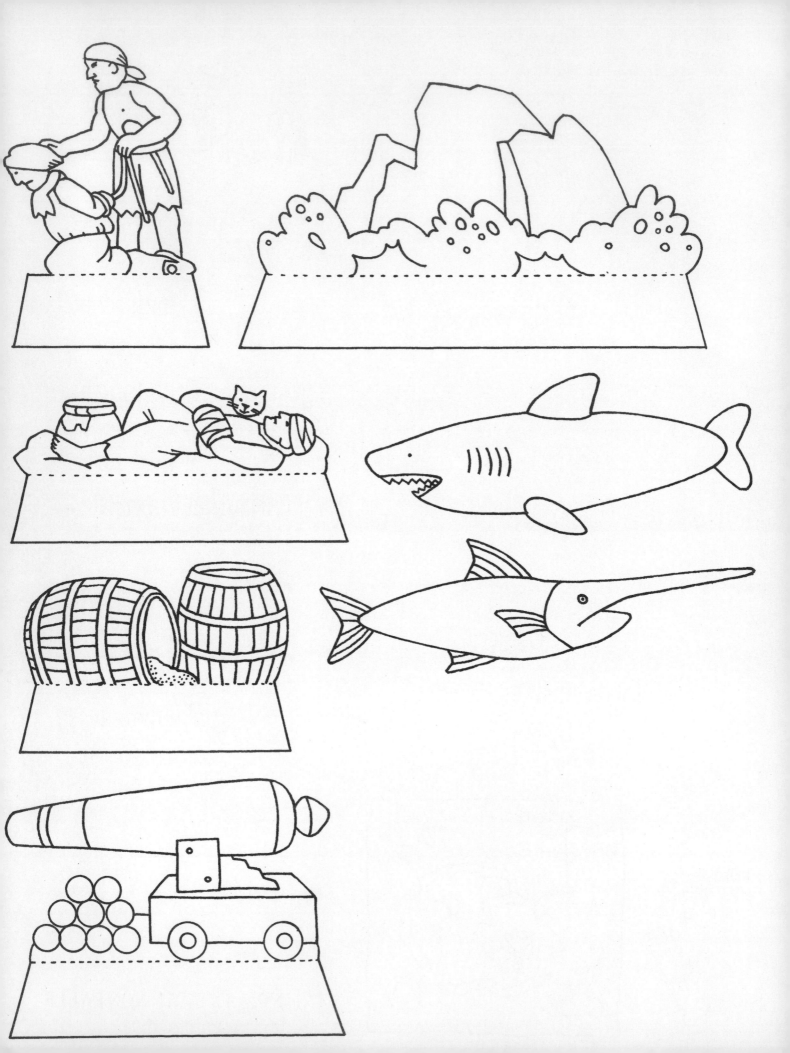

CAPTAIN

PIRATE

PIRATE

FIGHTING

COOK

CUT-THROAT PIRATES

PIRATE

PIRATE

PRISONER

PIRATE

PIRATE

FIGHTING

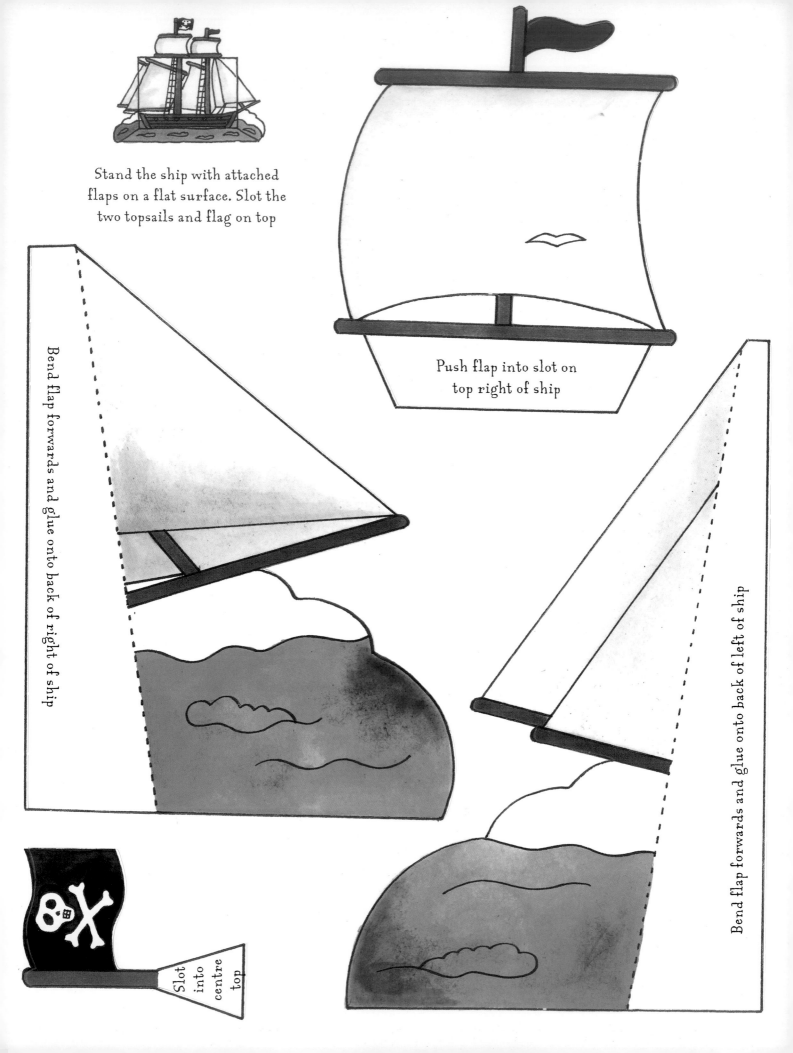

Stand the ship with attached
flaps on a flat surface. Slot the
two topsails and flag on top

Push flap into slot on
top right of ship

Bend flap forwards and glue onto back of right of ship

Bend flap forwards and glue onto back of left of ship

Slot into centre top

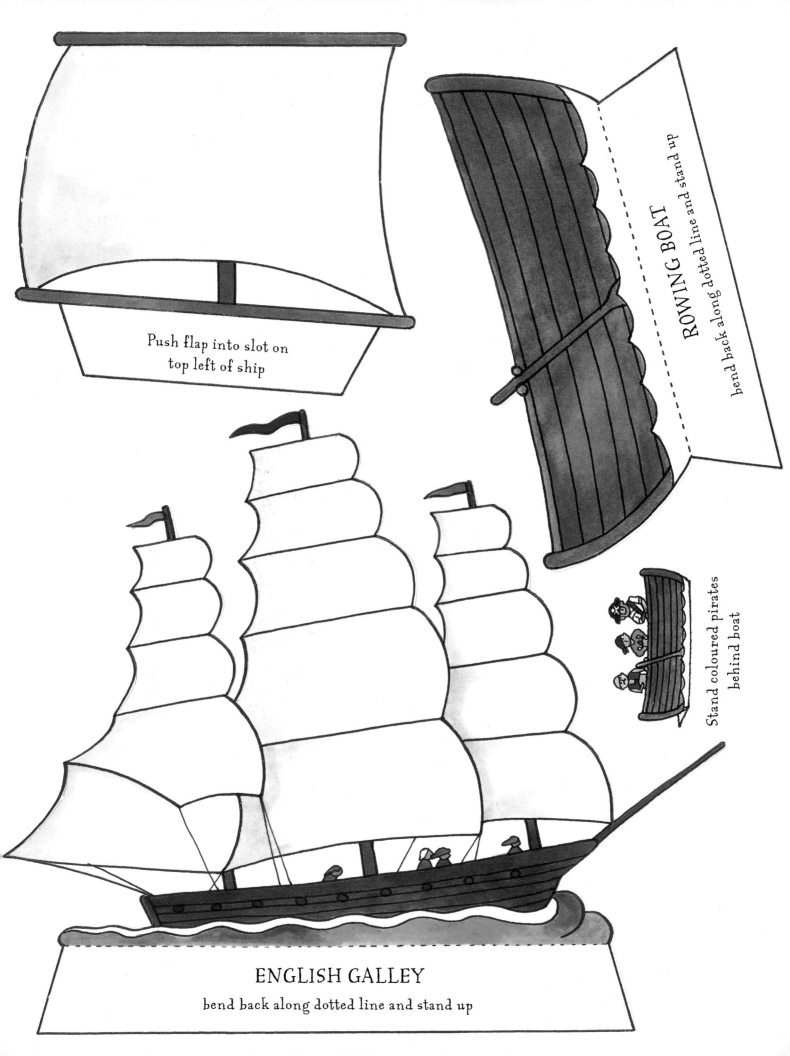

Push flap into slot on
top left of ship

ROWING BOAT
bend back along dotted line and stand up

Stand coloured pirates
behind boat

ENGLISH GALLEY
bend back along dotted line and stand up

TIDAL WAVE AND WRECK

WHALE

GIANT SQUID

SHARK

TREASURE CHEST

CAMP FIRE

GIANT JELLY FISH

LOOK-OUT

Lie the coloured and cut out pieces
without flaps on flat surface around
ship. Put some blue or green paper
down first if you have some.

TRADER

TRADER

TRADER

FIGHTING

When they weren't capturing trading ships, pirate ships had to be kept in good order. Decks had to be scrubbed, sails mended, cannons and other weapons cleaned. Pirates had to be fit, tough and have a 'head for heights'. They had to climb up the RIGGING in all weather conditions to look out for land or other ships.

Treasure islands

The stories of pirates burying treasure on islands are probably not true. It is more likely that sometimes ordinary people buried treasure to keep it hidden from pirates.

Pirates would have to WEIGH ANCHOR at islands or near the coast of the mainland to carry out repairs on their ships. They would also stock up on fresh drinking water and food.

One punishment for a pirate who had misbehaved was to be left alone on a desert island with nothing but a supply of water and a gun.

Make a treasure chest

Use an empty teabag or biscuit carton. Cover it in brown paper and leave it to dry. It doesn't have to be very neat.

Fill your treasure chest with chocolate money, real coins and jewellery.

Draw lines in black pen. Cut two thin strips of gold or silver paper and glue over three sides of the box.

Carefully cut the strip where the lid meets the side (so the lid can open).

Cut out a circle for the lock (draw keyhole) and two handles from gold or silver paper. Glue them onto the box.

Famous pirates

Blackbeard

His real name was Edward Teach but he was called Blackbeard because he wore his hair and beard long and stuck lighted tapers in his hair which belched out black smoke!

Born in England, he terrorised the east coast of America. When he was caught and beheaded, his head was tied to the bow of the ship.

Long John Silver

A character in the most famous pirate story of all, *Treasure Island*, by Robert Louis Stevenson, published in 1881. He had only one leg and used a crutch to move around.

Captain Hook

A wicked pirate in the book *Peter Pan* by J M Barrie, he had a hook in place of a hand after a crocodile had bitten it off!

Anne Bonny and Mary Read

Women were not allowed on pirate ships but these two disguised themselves as men. They sailed on the same ship in the Caribbean but were captured, tried and sentenced to death. But as they were both expecting babies, they went to prison instead.

Pirate myths

Over the years many books about pirates have been written. Often these gave a false impression of what a pirate's life was like by making it seem very exciting and glamorous.

Tales of pirates digging up buried treasure after following a map with X marking the spot and punishments such as 'walking the plank' (forcing a tied-up prisoner to jump into the sea to drown) probably hardly ever or never happened.

Pirates did not die old and rich. In reality they led tough and violent lives as criminals and often died young and poor.

Jolly Roger

The first pirate flag was red. Since then there have been many different designs. The black and white skull and crossbones is the best known flag today.

Using the instructions on the first page, make your own flag or patch for a hat.